"What I dream about is a proper potting shed." —Thomas C. Cooper

SMITH & HAWKEN

THE
POTTING
SHED

BY LINDA JOAN SMITH

PHOTOGRAPHS BY HUGH PALMER

WORKMAN PUBLISHING · NEW YORK

LIBRARY OF CONGRESS CATALOGING-IN-PUBLICATION DATA
SMITH, LINDA JOAN.
THE POTTING SHED/BY LINDA JOAN SMITH:
PHOTOGRAPHY BY HUGH PALMER.
P. CM.
ISBN 0-7611-0161-6
1. POTTING SHEDS.   2. PLANT PROPAGATION.
3. GARDENING.
I. TITLE.   II. TITLE: SMITH & HAWKEN
SB454.8.S63 1996
635.9'12—dc20   96-230
                                                     CIP

WORKMAN PUBLISHING
708 BROADWAY
NEW YORK, NY 10003-9555

MANUFACTURED IN THE UNITED STATES OF AMERICA

PRINTED ON RECYCLED PAPER

10 9 8 7 6 5 4 3 2 1

CONTENTS

WHERE *the* GARDEN BEGINS

Perhaps William Cobbett, writing to gardeners in the early nineteenth century, said it best: "There is yet one thing to notice in this laying out of the garden, namely, that there must be a shed to serve as a place for depositing tools, flower-pots, and the like; and also for the gardener to retire to in case of rain, and to do works there when they cannot do work out of doors. This is a very necessary part of the garden premises. . . ." In such a simple shed, now as then, the garden has its beginnings. We toil under its sheltering roof in sun and snow, daylight and darkness, when we are young and when we grow old, intent on a single task. To nourish. To cultivate. To garden.

Our reward is life itself.

THE POTTING SHED

Step into the potting shed and the hum of the everyday world dwindles into silence. The air is warm and smells of earth. Wood flats checkerboard the potting bench, terra-cotta pots tower in the corner like soup bowls on a kitchen shelf, and bins of soil beckon, their contents rich and deep.

Just above the potting bench, hand tools hang in rows as orderly as fence posts: trowels for digging, dibbers for transplanting, pruning shears for keeping errant shoots at bay. There are metal scoops for filling flats and pots, wood-rimmed sieves for banishing rocks and clods, and a trio of dented measuring spoons that clearly have seen better days.

Close by, sturdy wooden shelves clamber nearly to the rafters, offering up the staples of a gardener's pantry. Bags of meal, from bone to kelp. Amendments, from lime to sulfur.

Bottles of cayenne pepper spray and homemade insecticidal soap.

There are tins of brightly printed seed packets, enough for a dozen seasons (who can help but overbuy?), along with jars of small plain envelopes, each hand-labeled with names of seeds and the gardeners who shared them: Love-in-a-mist, Catherine Deeter, Summer 1994; *Nicotiana langsdorfii,* Mary Fisher, Fall 1995.

It is the unassuming contents of these packets that are the potting shed's symbolic heart. Seeds sprout and are nurtured here. Cuttings take root here. Tiny plants are potted on here—given larger quarters—and finally nudged into the garden.

But more than fledgling plants flourish beneath the potting shed's roof. Gardeners grow here, too. We learn and experiment. We dabble in artistry and alchemy, chemistry and biology. We tune ourselves to the song of the seasons, learn the rhythms of weeding and watering, and revel in the wealth of the harvest.

Sequestered from the accustomed demands of life, and focused on the task before us, our imaginations swell. The garden beyond the

Weathered shingles and giant urns lend character to a corner garden shed.

> *"The baskets were overflowing with flowers. I took them to the potting shed and thrust them into buckets of water."*
>
> —CECIL BEATON

door grows lush in an instant, and plum trees planted only yesterday droop beneath the weight of sun-warmed fruit. Visions for next season, and for countless years to come, unfold in vivid color to dazzle and entice. A new perennial bed against that old brick wall. A trellis of climbing roses beside the bedroom window. A fence of espaliered apple trees along the garden walk. No project seems too daunting to accomplish, and no time frame too long to wait for the imagined results.

Such dreams are not limited to the gardener who enjoys a full-fledged potting shed, perhaps with greenhouse attached. They come to us while we sift potting soil across the kitchen counter and onto the floor. They expand while we line up flats or punch out soil blocks in a corner of the garage, surrounded by stacks of newspapers ready for the recycler. They prosper while we recut the stems of heady roses

*P*otting alfresco suits many a gardener when sultry weather arrives. Here, a turquoise-rimmed
bowl stands in for an outdoor sink.

*F*or where the old thick laurels grow, along the thin red wall, You find the tool- and potting-sheds, which are the heart of all . . .

—RUDYARD KIPLING

under water in an old porcelain sink, rescued from the refuse heap and mounted just outside the back door, or while we mix potions on a makeshift table in the middle of the garden.

As gardeners we make do, improvising here, building there, until we have what we need to do the job at hand. Our potting bench may be as simple as a trio of weathered boards set on a pair of sawhorses or 50-gallon drums. Our piles of sand and wood ash may find a satisfactory home in plastic buckets, our cuttings may take root in cut-off milk cartons, and our empty pots may lie like ancient relics under the eaves of the house. So long as our plants thrive, we thrive, and are satisfied.

But somewhere along the way, on a day when everything from the curling tendril of a sweet pea to the worn handle of a favorite spade brings pleasure, we begin to conjure up a workspace that brings equal joy to our senses. Coaxing that vision into reality may take only the simplest act: clearing the old paint cans from the garage workbench so there's room to spread out flats, or installing a portable potting bench

A portable potting tray, rimmed on three sides to keep the mess contained, works readily on kitchen table or out in the garden.

OUT OF THE FLAT, ONTO THE FIRE ESCAPE

Plants that germinated during the Victorian and Edwardian eras had a wide choice of worldly situations, according to the *Cyclopedia of American Horticulture*, first published in 1900-02. "The first stage in the life of the plant is when the seedling is transplanted from the seed-bed," wrote Patrick O'Mara, author of the *Cyclopedia*'s article on potting. "It is then out of swaddling clothes and enters the ranks of its big brothers and sisters, on the way to making its bow in society; to live perchance in the window of the tenement or on the fire-escape; mayhap to refresh the eye of the patient in the sick-room; or to lose its identity in rows of its fellows in great glass houses where the blossoms are garnered and sent to market; perhaps to take its place in row upon row of its kind and make an arabesque pattern or gay border, and so delight the eye or regale the senses. . . ."

in the corner of the laundry room. Or, like our boundless garden visions, the desire for a pleasing place to pot may one day grow to shedlike proportions.

Exactly what shape that longed-for potting shed takes depends entirely on our individual whims. But it's likely the design and inspiration will lean heavily upon the potting and tool sheds that dot the English countryside, loved and used by generations of gardeners.

Perhaps that's due in some part to Beatrix Potter, who introduced many of us as children to Peter Rabbit and his heart-thumping exploits in Mr. McGregor's garden shed, with its fat green watering can and jumble of pots. Or it may be the influence of other writers.

THUMBS AND THIMBLES

Most clay flowerpots have changed little since the turn of the century, but their traditional names have gone the way of the leather garden hose and pony-drawn lawn roller. A pot 18 inches across used to be called a *two,* because two such pots could be made from a standard quantity of clay. A 9-inch pot was a *sixteen,* and a 3-inch pot a *sixty.* Anything smaller was a *thumb* or *thimble,* also known as a large or small *ninety.*

Long toms, with more upright proportions than a standard pot, were suited for growing plants with long taproots; *fern pans* were shallow clay vessels much like baking dishes, useful for potting small bulbs and other shallow-rooted plants.

Authors from Patricia Hall and Charlotte MacLeod to P.D. James and Graham Greene have elaborated on the potting shed's fertile, sometimes forbidden, and slightly mysterious charms; an unlikely preponderance of sinister, miraculous, and humorous fictional events seem to have occurred there.

Now that we have grown and become gardeners, the idea of such sheds pulls us like iron to a magnet. We are drawn to their simple structures, crafted without artifice from wood, slate, brick, and stone, or even galvanized steel and cement. We are seduced by their rugged substance; their humble grace and earthy integrity seem the antidote to much of modern life.

From that historic English tradition we both adopt and adapt, according to our tastes and circumstances.

Initially, we are like birds seeking a ready-made spot to nest, laying claim to any remotely usable site. The 1920s garage that's too cramped for cars. The 1950s pool house, deserted since the kids moved away. The 1970s chicken house whose tenants were evicted when eggs fell from dietary grace.

If no desirable roost can be found, we build one. It may be a bona-fide shed (a "slight" struc-

A shaded enclosure is a cool place to pot during summer's steamiest days; garden vines climb readily up its wooden gridwork.

POT'S PROGRESS

Warm as the earth from which they arise, decorative terra-cotta—or baked clay—urns have cradled plants since the days of the Egyptian pharaohs. But it wasn't until the 1700s that the utilitarian clay pot, so vital to indoor propagation, became widely available to nurserymen and gardeners. In 1706, Francis Gentil discussed its use in *Le Jardinier Solitaire,* where a simple rimless pot was illustrated. "Garden pot. To put Flowers in, that grow better so than in full earth. . . ." Such pots were thrown by the hand on a whirling potter's wheel, a standard method until the 1860s. At that time, American William Linton reportedly invented a machine for forming small clay pots; mechanized methods for molding larger pots followed.

Today, hand-thrown, rimless pots are back in vogue; gardeners prefer their vintage character and relish finding subtle ridges left by the potter's fingers.

classic potting shed, or have its own front porch or flagstone patio.

But whatever each potting shed's outward differences, inside are features agreed on by generations of gardeners.

The shed's hallmark, of course, is a potting bench, nearly a yard deep and as wide as space allows. It should stand at a convenient height, so the resident gardener can firm the earth in countless pots without tiring of the task, and should be bathed in light from overhead fixtures as well as from casement windows that swing open onto the glories and sweet breezes of the garden.

Beneath the bench, like flour bins in a Hoosier cabinet, should be galvanized tubs or built-in wood compartments for storing a season's worth of soil-mixing supplies. Although water can be hauled in from the garden faucet, a broad sink set into the potting bench, with a gooseneck faucet and a flexible hose and sprayer, is well worth the expense of the plumbing; it simplifies the filling of watering cans, eases the sprinkling of thirsty plants, and makes

ture according to definition), nailed together from scavenged wood and windows. It may be a substantial shingled cottage, designed by an architect to complement the style of our house. It may combine the functions and features of a greenhouse or lathhouse with those of a

Cast aside like old shoes, terra-cotta pots await the coming of an attentive and organized gardener.

short work of scouring even the largest garden pots. Light and air, earth and water—these are a gardener's friends.

In addition, there must be hooks and racks for hanging every fork, spade, hat, and smock; drawers or baskets for stashing copper plant tags, garden shears, and pruning knives; and shallow shelves for keeping boxes, bags, and bell-shaped cloches within sight and easy reach. Some shelves should be slatted, so dirt from muddy clogs and kneepads falls through to the floor; others should be like broad cupboards without doors, perfect nooks for caching awkward sprayers and watering cans, or for stacking heavy pots.

If space is ample and desire dictates, the potting shed holds still more. There's a flower press, still clutching brilliant remnants of last year's garden between its wooden plates. There's a growing table with fluorescent lights, and a chubby old refrigerator, chock-full of chilling bulbs. There are pegs along the rafters for hanging bundles of just-picked herbs and everlasting flowers, or for suspending bags of drying

Like the best nineteenth-century potting sheds, this shed's form and beauty spring directly from its function.

For an old-fashioned but practical touch, build in open-front wood bins beneath the potting bench for storing potting-soil mixes. Keep the soil from falling out with horizontal wood slats that slide down into place across the front of each bin; as potting work progresses and the soil level falls, the slats can be removed one by one.

seed heads that have yet to drop their harvest. And there are cases for journals and favorite garden books, baskets for catalogs, and a sunny corner for a welcoming wicker chair, complete with cushioned footstool.

There may even be a small woodstove or fireplace (or at the very least, a heater), so that the shed and its pleasures beckon even in the midst of winter. We seek refuge there, while the garden sleeps.

But soon we will tap small brown seeds from their paper packets. The first leaves of the seedlings will unfold, like smooth green wings, and tiny plants will begin their journey upward from the earth.

Life starts here.

Such is the lure of the potting shed.

THE PLEASURES *of the* POTTING SHED

What a playhouse or tree fort is to a child, a potting shed is to a gardener. Shielded in the leafy embrace of the garden, it is a carefully guarded hideaway. Alone there, we can dress as we please, act as we please, and play as we please. No grown-ups allowed.

If we are messy, no one will tell us to clean up. If we are neat, no one will disturb our order. We invent our own bylaws; the conventions of the outside world do not apply.

Dirt, for instance, is a welcome guest. In the house, mud and sand are turned away like unworthy beggars at the door, but in the potting shed we give them a warm reception. We load the bins beneath the potting bench with compost, peat moss, and aged manure, then mix and mold a gardener's brand of mud pies by the dozen. The dampened soil trails down our shirt front and onto the floor, but no matter. More will soon be tracked in from the garden.

Our clothes, too, are on friendly terms with dirt. When we head for the garden and potting shed, we dress down rather than up, casting off adult constraints for garments as carefree as the playclothes of our youth. Canvas pants with built-in kneepads, or a pair of sweatpants too unsightly for the gym. An old wool pullover or a loose cotton smock. A baggy tee shirt, and baggier shorts. Slip-on clogs, or battered tennis shoes without their laces. They are roomy and comfortable, no matter how we sit or twist or bend.

Other clothes wait for us in the shed itself: rain slickers, barn jackets, aprons to hold our garden tools, knee-high rubber boots for slogging through the mud. Hanging alongside are extra shirts and holey sweaters, shrugged off in the heat of summer and ready to warm us in the cool of fall. Like sachets, they soak up and

To encourage the growth of moss on new terra-cotta pots, brush them with a mix of one part active yogurt (plain, not flavored) and two parts water. Brush again with plain water after two weeks. Repeat process if needed.

then release the shed's familiar scent: drying lavender mingled with withered roses, manure overlaid with compost, sun-warmed creosote blended with the musty tang of potting soil. It is a potent elixir, an earthy essence that greets us when we enter and clings to us like perfume when we leave. For those of us raised at a gardener's knee, a moment's inhalation triggers an avalanche of memories.

The potting shed also revives our native curiosity, our youthful quest to know and understand. Like a child poring over a hand-wide patch of grass, fascinated by the minia-

" I like it 'ere. It smells like my dad's shed on the allotment."

—P. D. James
Shroud for a Nightingale

Reminders of summer, everlasting flowers litter a potting bench cobbled together from odds and ends of wood (above). Similar blossoms dry above a sheltered outdoor bench (opposite).

ture world concealed among the blades, at the potting bench we study life up close. We learn of monocots and dicots, radicles and plumules. We discover which plants feed upon a seed beneath the earth and which push the seed case forth, like a swim cap on their heads. We watch the seedlings of foxglove develop their first translucent hairs and marvel at the shimmer of the fledgling viola leaves, each waterplump cell a microscopic gem.

To the two-year-old's oft-repeated "Why?" we add "What?" and "How?" and "When?" Like junior scientists, we capture one of the caterpillars that's been gnawing the nasturtiums and clip the rose leaf with the mysterious purple spots, then carry them into the potting shed. Examined under magnifying glass or Coddington, successfully identified and noted, each is a clue to the mysteries of the garden.

Some days, we experiment, brewing odd concoctions of fish emulsion and seaweed,

Friendly blooms plucked from a summer border cool their heels in a bucket of water on the potting shed floor. Many gardeners shelve vases and flower frogs next to the potting bench, then clip and arrange flowers there before taking them into the house.

MOVING UP

To grow and thrive, potted plants need to be shifted from smaller to larger containers as their roots expand and exhaust available soil nutrients. To determine when it's time for a move, place one hand over the top of the pot with the plant's stem between your fingers. Turn the pot upside down and tap its rim down on the edge of the potting bench. The plant should slide out, soil and all. If only a few roots show through the soil, the plant's present home is fine. If the roots have begun to wrap around the outside of the soil, prepare for a shift to bigger quarters.

Rub off the old potting soil from the top of the plant's root ball, then choose a new pot one size larger than the last one. Keep the drainage hole from becoming clogged by covering it with a curved potsherd, then add fresh potting soil. Set in the plant and fill in with fresh soil around the sides and top. The plant should sit at the same soil level in its new home as in its original pot, with space left below the pot's rim for water to pool. Firm the soil with your thumbs, and by rapping the bottom of the pot firmly against the potting bench.

blending ground corn cobs into our potting soil, building a miniature hotbed full of chicken manure alongside the potting bench. We learn that the verb "to garden" means paying close attention, giving seedlings and cuttings what they need when they need it, rather than doling out water, food, light, and care according to whim or an arbitrary schedule. Taught by the waxing and waning of our plants in the one-room schoolhouse of the potting shed, we grow

ever more adept at enhancing life, and discard those practices by which it is diminished.

The garden isn't the only beneficiary of our education. In the potting shed, we arrange a nosegay of bright-faced pansies or force a pot of freesias to lift the flagging spirits of a neighbor. We fill a basket with buxom tomatoes, pungent basil, and freshly dug garlic for the brother who adores bruschetta, or polish globes of purple eggplant for the cousin who pines for baba ghanoush. We wrap our prize Asian pears in tissue paper and offer them up to visitors like the coveted apples of the Hesperides, then bind ribbons around the brittle stems of straw-flowers, forming everlasting bouquets for everlasting friends. There is joy in the giving.

To fellow gardeners we offer up a living bounty: the extra seedlings of our chili peppers, rooted cuttings from our pinks or verbena, divisions of our yarrow or mint. In return, they share their treasures, bringing pots of euphorbia or hellebore, carex or hosta. Our garden beds, like a family tree, form a record of our kinship.

A potting shed is a home away from home: part place to propagate, part office, part lunchroom (left), and part catchall for the detritus of a gardener's life (opposite).

Cutouts of a crow, goose, and other winged creatures populate the front of a wood-sided potting shed, equipped with a Dutch door for a wider view of the garden.

PLAYING IN THE DIRT

Making your own planting mixtures is akin to baking a cake from scratch. It takes a bit more work, but it's nice to know just what ingredients make those seedlings or transplants thrive.

Seed-starting mix: Mix equal amounts of horticultural-grade vermiculite, sharp sand or perlite, and Canadian milled peat moss. (This mixture contains no nutrients for plants, but it's perfect for germinating seeds. Once seedlings develop their first true leaves, you'll need to prick them out into a richer mix, or feed them each week with dilute fish emulsion or manure tea.)

Potting-soil mix: Sieve one part finished garden compost or leaf mold and blend it with one part Canadian milled peat moss and one part sharp sand or perlite. For a heavier texture, add one part commercial potting soil.

But we also retreat to the potting shed when our altruism falters. We leave the portable phone behind, forsake the ringing doorbell, forgo our visits and errands. We seek solitude, and the potting shed provides it. We read the newspaper and drink our morning coffee. We write, to meet a deadline for a book or newsletter, or to share thoughts with distant friends.

We sit with our feet up, and stare out the window at the changing sky.

Surrounding us are objects we cherish, displayed like artworks on wall or shelf: tattered garden books, a worn spade, a trio of antique wire flower frogs, a wacky handmade weeder picked up at a yard sale. Their quiet company connects us with the spirit and wisdom of the gardeners who preceded us. We look at their belongings, and wonder about their lives.

Imperceptibly at first, then undeniably, our wandering thoughts return to the garden. Our palm longs for the handle of the trowel, our foot for the tread of the shovel. The potting shed has worked its magic.

We head forth, eager to set out the transplants of cosmos and snapdragons that linger in the cold frame. The earth is warm and moist. We cast our gloves aside and sift it, like gold, through our fingers. A blue jay keeps us company while we work, poking around in the diggings, squawking like a boom box.

Hours later, we return to the house, dragging our feet like a reluctant child called home at the fall of dark, late on a summer's evening.

The knees of our pants are stained with green. We wear the dirt beneath our nails like a badge of honor.

THE TRADITION
of the
POTTING SHED

Time has stepped lightly in the potting shed, leaving little trace of its passing. Much of what we do there, as well as the building's form and furnishings, has been little changed for centuries. It is a humble yet hallowed hall: a monument to the perseverance of gardeners past and a testament to present pleasures.

One of the earliest illustrations of such a structure appeared late in the 1600s, in a German volume on farming and gardening by W. H. von Hohberg. Hohberg's shed was a cozy affair with windows, a pair of work-tables, and familiar garden implements from a wheelbarrow to a watering pot. Most of us could walk right in and get to work.

Similar garden work sheds or storage rooms probably existed even earlier; where else did the fourteenth-century monks at Abingdon Abbey, for instance, stash their spades, shovels, ladders, saws, rakes, trowels, seed baskets, and sieves? But it wasn't until the nineteenth century that the potting shed—as a well-equipped place to start seeds, pot up cuttings, and pot on plants, as well as carry out other garden-related tasks—became a customary part of garden life.

Until that time, gardeners generally had sown seeds or rooted cuttings directly in the garden, rather than in flats and pots indoors. A potting shed was simply not required. But as soon as greenhouse plant culture became a way of life (the result of a long influx of exotic heat-loving species from abroad), gardeners came to need a place to pot.

Potting sheds, or "working" sheds, could be found on large nineteenth-century estates alongside other "economical" buildings, from toolsheds and wheelbarrow sheds to mushroom, seed-drying, and rhubarb-forcing sheds. Known collectively as the back sheds, these sturdy stone lean-tos often were located just over the kitchen-garden wall from the culinary hothouses where melons, cucumbers, and grapes

The term "potting shed" seems to have come into use in the 1840s, but in an 1880s garden dictionary compiled by George Nicholson, curator of the Royal Botanic Gardens at Kew, no entry for potting sheds appeared. By that date, Nicholson assumed his readers knew all about them. "Tool Shed and Potting Shed, terms in frequent use, are self-explanatory," he wrote.

ripened despite cool weather. Especially in winter, gardeners could carry out chores in the back sheds while tending the greenhouse furnaces and profiting from their warmth.

"The part of these sheds more particularly set apart for working ought to be made perfectly light, and well aired by having numerous windows," wrote John Claudius Loudon

"Potting is a very nice operation; it should always be done (as it very frequently is not) in the most careful manner possible."
—WILLIAM COBBETT (1833)

*O*ld shears (opposite) find a home on the potting shed wall. Scouring stacks of pots like those above once was the job of a crock boy, who also "crocked" pots in preparation for planting.

in his widely read *Encyclopaedia of Gardening,* published in the 1820s. "Along these [should be] a range of benches or tables, for potting cuttings or bulbs, sowing seeds, preparing cuttings, numbering tallies. . . . making baskets, wattled hurdles, and a great variety of other operations. . . ."

Loudon also described a hybrid garden shed, suitable for modest plots: "In small gardens, where there are no hothouses, one small building is generally devoted to all the purposes for which the office, seed, tool, and fruit rooms, and working sheds, are used. This should be fitted up with some degree of attention to the various uses for which it is designed, and a fireplace never omitted."

The potting shed had come of age.

Both estate-size potting sheds and their multipurpose offspring saw heavy use from the 1830s on, as estate gardeners, then middle-class villa gardeners, indulged in the Victorian craze for tender bedding plants. Throughout

Brick-sided bins tucked beneath a well-worn potting bench keep bulk potting-soil ingredients within reach, while drawers cache smaller quantities of wood ash, broken pieces of pots, brick dust, and more.

MAKING DO

Recycling is far from a new idea in the garden and potting shed. In *The Book of Garden Management,* first published in 1862, Samuel Orchart Beeton suggested that his readers make drawers from old crates, then mount them beneath the potting bench for holding silver sand, peat, loam, coconut fiber, crocks, and the like.

"Rough boxes, such as those in which tinned lobster and salmon and Swiss milk are sent to this country, will answer the purpose as well and better than those made by a carpenter, because they cost little, and can be renewed at pleasure," the author wrote. "All that is necessary is to put up a framework to suit the size and to furnish runners on which the boxes may be drawn out and pushed in as required."

the century, gardeners working in the potting shed sowed endless flats of vibrant salvias from Mexico or petunias from Brazil, shifted them up from pot to pot, then raised them to flowering size under glass before bedding them out in decorative parterres. Some estate gardens produced as many as forty thousand transplants for a single growing season.

With the end of the Victorian era, however, contrived bedding schemes slowly fell

From the mid-nineteenth century on, large multi-winged greenhouses often included a potting room under their soaring glass roofs. Such work spaces usually were situated next to the boiler room or over the boiler cellar for warmth.

out of favor, upstaged in part by subtle yet glorious perennial gardens that flowered, in natural succession, from spring until fall. "Experience has taught me to throw overboard all tender plants," wrote author William Robinson in the preface to the 1921 edition of *The English Flower Garden,* in which he likened annual-filled parterres to "a bad carpet." In Robinson's opinion, labor-intensive greenhouses, too, could go.

But twentieth-century gardeners still required a sheltered spot to store their tools and supplies, as well as to germinate seeds, root cuttings, and pot up tiny plants for growing on in the garden. For that purpose, gardeners converted old stone privies or built simple wood potting sheds, coated with creosote to ward off decay. Others transformed abandoned outbuildings or, if the climate

allowed, built lath-shaded potting benches outdoors. Even gardeners of British allotments (small leased plots where city dwellers could grow fruits and vegetables) built tiny sheds, cobbled together from odds and ends of lumber and recycled windows and doors—a tradition that continues.

In America, the storage of tools—rather than the seeding of pots and flats—became the primary focus of many garden sheds, but their garden function was largely the same as that of their English counterparts. In the October 1912 issue of *The Garden Magazine,* Phil M. Riley outlined the building and uses of an attractive toolshed, but complained that some gardeners had indulged in decorative excess. "An inordinate desire for picturesqueness has led some of us to such extremes, for instance, as Japanese pagoda tool sheds . . . about our staid New England Colonial residences," he wrote.

Upright and solid as an ancient oak, this nineteenth-century shed includes a sizable loft for seasonal storage of winter squashes, onions, and drying herbs and flowers, while downstairs, wheel hoes, garden carts, and the like have ample room to roll.

*P*ots, pots, and more pots are piled from floor to rafters in an old-time pot shed, a handy adjunct to the potting shed itself.

"The front wall, halfway, is furnished with shelves for placing shreds and nails, rope yarn, tallies, flower pegs, whetstones, rubber or scythe-stones, and many other small articles."

—MR. BARNES OF BICTON GARDENS

Other gardeners, however, used more restraint. "I had thought about and planned my ideal tool-house for thirty-five years," wrote Anna Gilman Hill in *Forty Years of Gardening,* published in New York in 1938. Her garden house, which bore all the hallmarks of the best English potting sheds, was a "demure" fieldstone cottage of 12 by 14 feet, with a table where she often sat in a cushioned chair to draw up garden plans, consult her favorite reference books, or have "a restful cup of tea." What once was a place of toil for hired laborers had become a rejuvenating refuge for the dedicated home gardener.

For most Americans, though, the potting shed tradition never took hold; there was little need for such a structure in the typical

CROCKED AND POTTED

"For the purpose of providing drainage, every gardener keeps by him a store of fragments of broken pots and saucers, oyster shells, and even broken pieces of soft brick," wrote Samuel Orchart Beeton in *The Book of Garden Management* (1862). Beeton and other writers of the time advised filling as much as one-quarter of each pot with pot fragments, or crocks, arranged with the largest pieces on the bottom. "The pot being crocked, it is considered desirable by some to place a little moss or cocoanut fibre, or even a few leaves, over the crocks before putting in the soil," Beeton continued.

If gardeners were short on accidental fragments, they took hammer to pot during the winter months; nurseries in the early twentieth century used a crock-breaking machine. American nurseryman Peter Henderson, writing in 1901 in *Gardening for Pleasure,* advocated a different method. "We ourselves now use a wad of the 'excelsior' as drainage for all pots under seven inches, and nothing else, dispensing entirely with potsherds." Excelsior, he noted, was a "new packing material."

American yard. After World War II, Victory gardens gave way to suburban lawns, supermarkets supplied blemish-free fruits and veg-

The roof of Gertrude Jekyll's turn-of-the-century potting shed at Munstead Wood was thatched with "hoop-chip," left over from the local production of barrel hoops.

etables, and nurseries offered up all the transplants of petunias and zinnias a homeowner could want. A closet-size sheet-metal shed or a corner of the garage was all one needed to house the lawn mower, a can of gas, a rake, and some hedge clippers—why fuss with more?

Across the Atlantic, the expansive estate gardens of the nineteenth century also gave way to modest plots surrounding newly built post-war dwellings. Yet England remained primarily a land of gardeners, as attached to their tradition of garden sheds as to their scones and crumpets. To many of us raised

A pristine potting shed stands on feet of stone (right). In Victorian times, the stone floors of potting and tool sheds like the one opposite were "neatly swept up every night, the last thing, and washed every Saturday thoroughly."

on Bermuda grass, it seems they took the better path.

But now we embark on a parallel journey. We have shrugged off the typical suburban yard, with its lawn and collar of landscape shrubs, like a threadbare coat that no longer keeps us warm. In its place, we gather together strands of gardening tradition, from the swept-dirt gardens of rural Texas to the cottage gardens of the English countryside, and weave them into a sanctuary of our own making.

More and more often, a potting shed stands at its heart.

THE TOOLS *of the* POTTING SHED

S ince ancient times, when gardeners cultivated the earth with primitive hoes and digging sticks, tools have been what "enables the hand to obey the brain," in the words of legendary English gardener Gertrude Jekyll. Without them we would be like biblical Adam and Eve: permanently barred from the glories of the garden. Tools are our keys to the kingdom: our "open sesame" to the treasures of the earth.

Gardeners look upon tools with a well-deserved sort of reverence. In the potting shed, spades, hoes, forks, and rakes hang on the walls like icons: their honed blades gleaming in the sunlight, their teeth straight and bright, their upright handles a triumph of order over chaos.

Such order has long been a part of the garden ethos. "Have a place for everything, and everything in its place;—kept in good condition, and at all times put away clean," advised Mr. Barnes of England's Bicton Gardens in the middle of the previous century, and to this commandment—and its attendant rituals—we religiously adhere. Scrape mud from spades and shovels before it dries and hardens. Wipe tool blades with vegetable oil to prevent corrosion and rust. Empty watering cans before

A Keen Edge

When time is short and the garden beckons, it's tempting to wait for a rainy day to hone your hoe or sharpen a spade. But dull blades, like dull minds, dampen the pleasures of the work; the whisper of the spade as it slices cleanly through the earth is traded, instead, for an extra ounce of sweat from the gardener.

Give a tool its proper edge, however, and it will perform with ease. Most fine garden tools come with the proper bevel when new, and this should be maintained with each sharpening. Secure spades, forks, or hoes in a vise, if possible, and sharpen with a mill bastard file. Take the file in both hands and push it across the beveled edge, sliding it away from you and sideways in quick, short strokes as you work. When the edge has been renewed, give the back side of the blade a few light strokes.

Pruners, knives, axes, and scythes require a finer edge, and are best sharpened with a whetstone. For starters, have these tools honed by an expert (check in the Yellow Pages under "Sharpening Services"). Watch how it's done, then practice up in the privacy of the potting shed.

storing. Sharpen hoes after hard use. All of these rites, passed on by earlier gardeners, unite us and serve us well. We stop short, of course, of fining ourselves—or each other—for transgressions (the way Mr. Barnes did his workmen) when we leave our scuffle hoe propped against the back fence or our muddy trowel lying in the herb garden. The guilt that lies in abusing a good tool is punishment enough.

And as much as we can, we do own *good* tools. The very elements from which they're made, and the methods by which they're assembled, inspire our devotion. Ash for handles, hard and straight of grain. Carbon steel, forged into stalwart blades. Solid socket construction. Over time, we've learned that buying a cheap trowel or hoe is a false economy; it's far cheaper to buy the best than to buy a dozen flimsy versions. Good tools, well cared for, may very well outlast us, and survive to cultivate future Edens we will never see.

The true rewards of such able instruments, however, are clearly in the present. There are few satisfactions as keen as wielding a well-made tool that's perfectly matched to the present job. The weight is right. The fingers wrap comfortably around the handle, worn smooth as silk. The blade is sharp and true. The

*R*etired to the potting shed rafters, well-worn grass hooks recall the gardens of another time.
When meadow grasses encroached on the garden, one swipe made short work of the interlopers.

"My hoe as it bites the ground revenges my wrongs, and I have less lust to bite my enemies. In smoothing the rough hillocks, I soothe my temper."

—Ralph Waldo Emerson

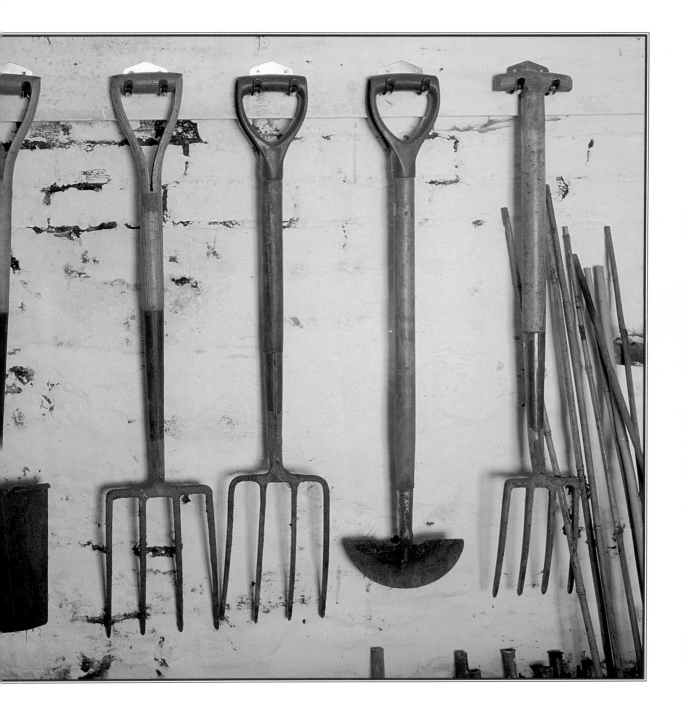

Increase the life and resiliency of wooden tool handles by sanding off their coat of varnish and rubbing them periodically with boiled linseed oil. When the oil dries, buff the wood with fine steel wool for a satin-smooth finish.

proper tool makes short work of rehabilitating the most recalcitrant garden bed, snipping the thorniest roses, or bringing errant hedges into line, all without blistering the hand or breaking the back of the gardener.

It is certainly possible, as J. C. Loudon, author of *An Encyclopaedia of Gardening,* observed in the 1820s, to get by with only a few basic implements: he suggested the spade, the dung fork, and the rake, along with "one or two instruments for pruning trees or gathering crops." But even in Loudon's time, the number of useful garden tools was, as

Some gardeners make labels for their tools as well as their plants, to ensure each one has a home (opposite). Others fill the space between wall studs with hangers and clips to ensure an orderly array (right), or hook hoes and rakes over the wall's exposed top plate.

he put it, "greatly extended and diversified."

In fact, the implements he pictures include far *more* items than most gardeners today will ever own, and lack only a handful of today's standards and novelties. Few among us, for instance, possess a wire besom, "used for sweeping gravel paths which have become mossy," or a haulm-barrow, an open wicker box useful for carrying litter, leaves, and "haulm": the spent growth of beans, peas, and potatoes.

But as our gardens grow, so do the number of tools stored in the potting shed. Most

CLEANING AND STORING TOOLS

Like a favored cast-iron skillet, tools benefit from regular cleaning and seasoning. Before pulling off your garden boots, scrape or brush off the damp earth that clings to the blades of shovels, trowels, forks, and hoes using a stick, spatula-like "wood man," or stiff brush. Wipe the blades clean, then coat them lightly with vegetable oil to keep rust at bay.

If rust already has attacked your trowel or weeder, scour the blade with a pliable sanding block or stiff wire brush until the steel gleams through, then give it a protective oil coating.

Once tools are clean, hang them up off the floor on wooden peg racks or hooks, or with handle holders designed for gripping straight handles. The blades of the tools will stay sharp longer, and your rakes and hoes won't trip you up as you traipse back and forth from the garden.

"'If I have a spade,' she whispered, 'I can make the earth nice and soft and dig up weeds. If I have seeds and can make flowers grow the garden won't be dead at all —it will come alive.'"

—FRANCES HODGSON BURNETT
THE SECRET GARDEN

born weeds; the hoe has retained that vital garden role to this day. "This is the implement which should be most frequently in the gardener's hand," Loudon advised 1820s gardeners, "for the surface of the soil scarcely can be too frequently stirred." Other standbys include steel garden rakes, cultivators with three or four curved fingers (once known as prong or claw hoes), hand cultivators, and weeders.

DIGGING: Tools for digging, turning, and lifting the earth include the familiar garden spade and shovel, both used in ancient China and during Roman times, as well as the garden fork and trowel. All were greatly improved during the nineteenth century when carbon steel replaced blades of iron; now some

essential are implements for easing the following labors, a quest that has challenged gardeners and toolmakers since planting first began.

CULTIVATING: Even Stone Age gardeners needed implements with which to scratch a furrow in the earth or chop at the roots of stub-

*T*ools, flowerpots, and bamboo poles mingle in an abstract composition on a canvas of white-painted wall; such painted or white-washed interiors brighten a gardener's potting shed tasks.

gardeners opt for low maintenance, non-rusting stainless steel.

CUTTING AND PRUNING: Unlike hoes and garden forks, cutting tools take "more skill than physical force" to operate, according to Loudon. His observation was astute: each cut of the pruning shears shapes the future of the garden, for better or for worse. The earliest pruner was a sharp knife ("Every working-gardener ought to carry one of these knives in a side-pocket on his thigh," he wrote). Today's must-haves include pruning shears, flower shears or scissors, loppers, hedge shears, and a pruning saw, though more specialized options—along with traditional garden knives—abound.

WATERING: A watering can, wrote Francis Gentil in 1706, "imitates the rain, falling from the heavens": a God-like feat even the earliest gardeners tried to perform. They used their fingers to sprinkle gentle water drops; in later centuries, perforated clay pots and metal cans baptized thirsty plants. Today, although sturdy hoses, sprayers, sprinklers, and drip-lines have taken over most watering chores,

watering-can types abound; traditional copper or galvanized-steel watering cans in nineteenth-century styles remain garden favorites.

There are other helpful tools, of course; essential for some gardeners and extraneous for others. There are flexible bamboo or wire rakes for neatening lawns or gathering leaves and garden debris, and garden lines for laying out neat rows of carrots and beets. There are dibbers for poking holes in the earth, open-centered bulb planters for digging burrows for daffodils, and homemade wooden floats for tamping down soil in flats.

Each is a means to an end, enabling us to do more than our bodies, unaided, could possibly accomplish. But it is not the tools that make the garden. Without our minds, eyes, hands, and hearts, the tools lie still as stones.

They need us. We need them. The garden needs us both.

Tools above, pots below, is the rule in this hardworking shed (opposite). Wood pegs cradle well-worn tool handles (right).

SEASONAL JOYS *and* TIMELY LABORS

In the potting shed, the conventional counting of minutes and hours bears no relation to our work. We tell time, instead, by the rhythm of the seasons: we move to a cadence of tasks and pleasures that draws us forward, no matter what our climate, from one garden season to the next. Now is the time to start the tomato seeds. Now is the time to transplant the peppers and lemon geranium cuttings and to weed the vegetable beds. Now is the time to dry the rosebuds for potpourri. Now is the time to replace the rake handle, make new plant labels, force the narcissus bulbs, pore over the seed catalogs. We labor by the garden's clock; we can feel its gentle ticking in our bones.

SPRING'S TENDER RITES

S pring comes early behind the closed doors of the potting shed. Gardeners cannot wait for it to arrive in its own good time, creeping slowly through the perennial beds; winter has been too long and the hunger for green is too great. Weeks before the soil outside has lost its icy chill, or heart-shaped leaves have clothed the naked lilacs, we urge the season along.

Bent over the potting bench, with heater or wood stove blazing, we tuck seeds into foot-wide fields of earth. Days pass. We wait and water. Below their blanket, beyond our knowing, the seeds soften and swell, heavy with awakened life. Then, ever so quietly, the white forerunners of stem and root force their way through the seeds' outer coats and blindly begin to explore the dark.

We wait some more, poring over our bench-top plots each day like hopeful scientists over their petri dishes, searching for the little hump or crack in the soil's surface that heralds the birth of a plant. Finally, just when we begin to question how a speck of a seed, shriveled and hard, could ever hold the essence of basil or pansy, pale green cotyledons, sprung from their cramped prisons, unfold and push their way into the light.

The season of growth has begun, and with it, our gardening passions quicken.

We are well prepared for our midwifing

GROWING UNDER COVER

Starting as early as the 1600s, gardeners coddled transplants, nurtured seedlings, and rooted cuttings beneath glass covers known as bell-glasses or cloches—miniature greenhouses that could be moved around the garden at will.

Today, reproductions of such simple plant protectors are popping up in vegetable and flower beds like weeds after a spring rain; even so, gardeners have few of the cloche choices available to their nineteenth-century counterparts. Along with four or five types of glass bells, domes, and cylinders, earlier gardeners could buy hand-glasses—cloche-like covers constructed from many small panes of glass set in angular frames of lead, copper, cast iron or wood. Some hand-glasses came with separate glass and metal bases; two or more could be stacked before the top went on to accommodate larger plants.

Those gardeners who couldn't locate commercially made hand-glasses or bell-glasses were advised to improvise by periodicals such as *Vick's Monthly Magazine.* Prompted one 1879 article: "The clever amateur will adapt the tumbler, the broken fruit jar, the cracked fish-globe, or other piece of glassware, to the service."

tasks. Before the first seed is sifted from its packet, we assemble favored instruments on the potting bench: stainless-steel scoops, wood-rimmed riddles for sifting compost, miniature dibbers, and more. We study the backs of seed packets and consult trusted authors for wise words on soaking seeds or nicking their impenetrable coats; we note germination times and plan the sequence of our planting; and we print out Latin and common plant names on tongue depressors, plastic picnic knives, or any other markers we have on hand, to better track our sowings. We sterilize flats and tamp them full

of seed-starting mix, soak odd little disks of peat until they plump, or eject soil blocks, like cubist mud pies, from their molds. Each ritual, reinforced by every season of seed-starting success, adds to our anticipation.

If we're organized and methodical, the potting bench takes on the no-nonsense look of a production line; if not, it is an earthy jumble. Either way, the work of hastening spring is soon accomplished.

Other tender labors follow. As waves of seedlings flex their first true leaves and stretch their roots, crowding each other in their flats, they demand to be pricked out to larger, less Spartan quarters. A rich mix of soil muddies the bench as we choose the sturdiest plantlets to be potted on, then gently transfer them from flats to cell packs and on to pots. Cramped cuttings, rooted last fall, get similar upgrades in living space.

*W*ell-mixed and moistened potting soil is swept into hillocks on the potting bench, ready for
careful firming around tender transplants or rooted cuttings (above). Wood flats (opposite)
have been a potting shed fixture since the nineteenth century.

Move seedlings germinated in nutrient-poor seed-starting mix to flats or cell-packs filled with potting soil soon after true leaves appear. Feed with a one-quarter-strength solution of liquid organic fertilizer every week or ten days.

Outside, meanwhile, the garden has begun to stir; spring has caught up with our indoor enterprises, seemingly in an instant. We make frequent forays from the shelter of the potting shed, afraid to miss a single moment. The thin sun warms our backs as we bend low to the ground, searching for signs of life. First the snowdrops, and then the daffodils and tulips poke their pointed green noses up above the earth's surface, testing the temperature. Buds begin to fatten on the apple trees, bushes wrap themselves in a bright green mist, and the first silver froth of artemisia lies on the ground like lace.

All is new, pristine, perfect. The slate is clean; any garden vision is now within our grasp. The winter of waiting is forgotten and the pace speeds up to suit our hopeful mood.

With door swung wide, the potting shed disgorges most of its contents: wheelbarrows, ladders, buckets and cloches, spades, rakes, and broad forks. We prune, pull mulch from perennial beds, sprinkle the bare dirt with composted manure and bonemeal. We trim out deadwood and hoe the first weeds. Out come the garden lines, and we mark off rows for carrots and radishes and early peas.

And then it's time for planting. The soil is warming, and the threat of frigid temperatures is past. Seedlings are shifted from their cozy spots in bright windows or the greenhouse to cold frames in the garden, in order to toughen their tender leaves and stems. New batches of seeds are poured from their packets like small brown gems, directly into furrows that corduroy the earth. We poke our trowels and dibbers into the

"For March, there come Violets, specially the Single Blue, which are the Earliest, the yellow Daffodil, the Daisy, the Almond-Tree in blossom . . ."

—SIR FRANCIS BACON (1625)

soil, giddily making homes for our transplants of beets and cabbages, lettuces and leeks, along with violas, stocks, campanulas, and foxgloves. Watered by gentle rains, the plants grow with abandon.

As if the tonic of the earth and air were not enough to stir our blood and set our limbs to jumping, soon we gather up fat bundles of frilled tulips, arcs of trembling bleeding hearts, the first bearded iris. Naked no longer, the green-leaved lilacs now are cloaked with blooms; we carry them into the potting shed to crush their woody stems and plunge them into water. Their honeyed scent intoxicates. It lingers while we work.

GARDEN BUILDING BLOCKS

Not all that's good in the garden has roots deep in the past. Soil blockers are relative newcomers to the potting shed but have won a host of converts.

These mechanisms for molding mixtures of sieved peat moss and compost come in three different sizes, allowing the gardener to eject, by releasing the spring handle, twenty perfect little cubes for starting seeds, four 2-inch blocks for starting seeds or growing seedlings, or one 4-inch block for nurturing larger transplants. If desired, the larger blocks can be formed to accommodate the next smaller size block or cube: pop the plantlet—soil cube and all—in the ready-made depression in the larger cube, and transplanting is complete.

Ejected in rows in a flat, the freestanding cubes are easy to monitor for moisture, allow ample oxygen to reach plant roots, and minimize transplant shock.

SUMMER'S
SWEET PURSUITS

O ne day it is cool in the garden, the next it is hot. Plants once garbed in emerald leaves, veined like the wings of dragonflies, have dressed themselves in opaque blue-green, a hue well suited to life in the sun. The pointed buds of tea roses have plumped like opera-house divas and are as heavily perfumed, while the hollyhocks have shot, like rockets, to the sky.

Color takes center stage in every row and bed: the crimson stalks of ruby chard, the jeweled magenta of cranesbill geraniums, the unearthly orange of nasturtium and California poppy. What once was sparse, pruned, and orderly, now is crowded and full of life: a fertile spectacle that commands our rapt attention.

As the season ignites, its shameless theatrics beckon, and we emerge from the shade of the potting shed costumed and equipped for our varied supporting roles.

First, we play the water bearer, quencher of thirst and delayer of drought. We wear a broad straw hat and heft our watering cans, sometimes two at a time. We tame the coiling hose, and monitor the emitters on the drip lines as they hiss and spit. We set sprinklers and timers, and adjust the gentle shower from our spray lance, then spread truckloads of mulch to maximize the effects of our efforts. The plants applaud.

Our next role is the warrior, destroyer of

*W*himsical painted pots enliven this lath-shaded potting center, where the family feline and a potted amaryllis are equally at home.

pests and guardian of the gate. We wear long sleeves and pants, and carry a sprayer. In the potting shed, we mix gallons of insecticidal soap, then set out saucers of beer to lure the slugs, and lace the apricot tree with shiny tinsel to discourage the birds. If the battle becomes pitched, we turn nature on herself and muster the forces of the praying mantis, the trichogramma wasp, the green lacewing, and the ladybug. As summer wears on, a fragile peace prevails.

Then comes our turn as the custodian: puller of weeds, pruner of spent blooms, turner of compost. We wear kneepads and carry thinning shears in our pocket; our back is strong and our pitchfork is always close at hand. In a posture of prayer, we plunge our fishtail weeder deep into the soil and lever out tap-rooted trespassers. We see how tenaciously spurge spreads, wearing spotted camouflage, and we rise to rout it with oscillating hoe or long-handled cultivator. We break for lemonade, then switch to lighter work— snipping the withered blossoms that sap strength from the penstemon, clipping the stray shoots on the boxwood, cutting back the scented geraniums—before we turn our takings into the dark and humid compost pile.

We also play the gatherer, master of the

TEATIME

On the largest English estates, one garden shed often was reserved solely for storing casks of liquid manure: "the most advantageous form in which fertilizers can be applied by the gardener to his crops," according to Johnson's *Dictionary of Modern Gardening* (1847).

The proportions for this magic brew varied with the main ingredient, from sheep's dung to guano from Peru. But no matter the recipe, the primary rule of use remained the same: "Give it weak, and often."

Today, concocting liquid manure is as simple as brewing a batch of sun tea. Scoop three to four shovelfuls of composted manure into a cloth or burlap bag, and tie it shut. Drop the bag into a plastic garbage can full of water and let it steep for a week or two, swirling daily if desired. Add the used bag to the compost pile, and serve the nutritious drink, diluted to the color of weak tea, to previously watered plants via your watering can.

harvest—a role coveted by all who answer the garden's casting call. Understudies are many: the neighbor who covets the tomatoes, the raccoons who raid the sweet corn, the children who gobble two berries for each one in their pails.

"*In spring and summer, isolated in the quiet of the trees and surrounded by bird song, it must, Dalgliesh thought, be an agreeable hiding place.*"

—P. D. JAMES
SHROUD FOR A NIGHTINGALE

As the day begins to cool, we arrive home from work and rush to the potting shed. We slip on clogs or tattered tennis shoes to trek down the garden rows, gathering quart baskets of raspberries, tiny heads of butter lettuce, string beans thin as a baby's finger. We slice through the base of weighty cabbages, tug beets from their earthy hollows, and hunt for zucchini among the rampant vines. Before delivering them to the kitchen, we bathe the garden's groceries in the potting shed sink.

In the morning, before the sun intensifies but after the dew has fled, we continue summer's harvest. Soon, the trug basket is brimful of oregano, rosemary, and tarragon ready to be tied with string and dangled from the potting shed's rafters. We make another foray, then scatter damask roses on screens in a dark corner of the shed to dry for potpourri. Yet another trip yields choice blossoms of four-o'clocks, coreopsis, and potentilla, gathered for the beauty of their forms, then layered in the potting shed's flower press. This winter, when snowflakes are the garden's only blooms, they will resurrect summer's glory.

Finally, after months of splendor, the pageantry begins to wane. The lettuce and cabbages have bolted and the color has been bleached from the petals of the flowers. It is now, when the afternoons are too hot for work and the enthusiasms of May and June have evapo-

THE KINDEST CUT

In early summer, gardeners litter the potting bench with cuttings of actively growing plants and poke them into sand-filled flats. Soon, the cuttings root and shoot forth new leaves. Later in the summer, with little work and less expense, the gardener has new plants of euphorbia, thyme, rosemary, salvia, lantana, and more, ready to be potted on or transplanted into the garden.

To root softwood (or green) cuttings, fill a clean flat with a mix of coarse sterile sand and vermiculite; moisten well. Using a clean sharp knife, take 2- to 4-inch cuttings of the recent growth on plants, cutting on a 45-degree angle, $\frac{1}{4}$ inch to $\frac{1}{2}$ inch below the lowest leaves. Include at least four leaves. Remove any flowers and all but the top few leaves. Dip just the cut end of the stem into rooting hormone. Poke a 1-inch-deep hole in the rooting medium, then insert the cutting and firm the medium around it. Cover the flat with a clear plastic cover to maintain high humidity; keep the flat moist and in bright but indirect sunlight. Transplant after new leaves sprout.

A *lath screen shades an outdoor bench from the full force of the sun's rays and protects potted
plants—and the gardener—from summer's withering heat.*

"Making the earth say beans instead of grass, —this was my daily work."

—HENRY DAVID THOREAU

rated, that the mantle of reviewer settles on our shoulders. We take our garden journal or notebook from the potting shed shelf (as informal as a yellow legal pad or as fancy as a brocade binder) and drop into a creaking wicker chair, on permanent loan from the front porch. We leaf through the pages littered with pictures clipped from catalogs, and filled with notes on the performance of each plant. We philosophize in print about the week's disappointments and pleasures—the sudden appearance of a new crop of aphids, the pair of mockingbirds that came to the birdbath while we hoed—then add reminders to our script for the coming garden year.

Summer potting takes place on a small table tucked in the shade outside this shed; pots of abutilon, foxglove, and nicotiana form a diminutive garden alongside (opposite). Tin cans fill in for pots on a rugged outdoor bench (above).

Plant more golden beets and fewer red ones. Order a new rose to replace the 'Conrad Ferdinand Meyer' rugosa that so readily succumbed to rust. Replace the faltering boxwood around the herb bed with germander, and watch carefully for mildew on the chocolate cosmos.

The breath of the garden wafts through the open windows. It is warm, heavy with the scents of sun-baked earth and fading flowers. In the cool of the potting shed, we weave it into our writings.

FALL'S BITTERSWEET GATHERINGS

The sun leans a fraction lower in the sky. The shadows stretch. Looking up from our watering and weeding, we suddenly notice the texture of the cornstalks and the brilliance of the dahlias, or that a wash of orange—imperceptible just yesterday—has tinted the rose hips. Autumn has arrived.

Soon, frost will wither the morning glories and blacken the basil. But for now, the fennel shoots forth a fountain of green. Crabapples cluster thick along their branches. Ornamental kale unfolds in frilled bouquets of purple and cream, and *frikartii* asters dance around the sedums. The sleek cedar waxwings, absent for a year, visit the berried cotoneasters in droves.

The potting shed, which cast forth its contents during the summer months, now gathers in the garden's lingering bounty. Stacks of bushel baskets carried into the garden return heavy with 'McIntosh' apples or 'Warren' pears, 'Yellow Finn' potatoes or acorn squash. Burlap sacks, sent forth to the bean vines, return plump with pintos that rattle in their papery pods, and buckets dispatched to the tomato vines come back brimming with crimson. Tubs of such treasures line up across the potting shed floor; preserved via freezer, canning kettle, and dehy-

HARBINGERS OF SPRING

When all the world is glazed in ice, paperwhite narcissus—seduced into early flowering—provide the perfect antidote to winter's somber ways.

1) Choose containers that are at least 4 inches deep, and that have drainage holes. Fill with potting soil to within 2 inches of the rims; arrange narcissus bulbs, tips up and evenly spaced, on top. Add more soil to cover the lower two-thirds of the bulbs. Water gently.

2) Place the potted bulbs in a cool room (50° to 55°F) for a week or two to develop roots. Keep the soil moist but not soggy.

3) When the roots have developed and bulbs have sprouted, place the containers in a sunny window to bloom, then shift to a location with bright indirect light. To keep the flower stems from leaning, rotate the pots regularly.

For continual blooms, start pots in succession; store the bulbs in paper bags in a cool dry spot until it's their turn for planting.

from the hearts of winter squash, cleanse the seeds of their orange flesh, and lay them on a fine mesh screen. We shake wrinkled black beads from the balloon-like capsules of love-in-a-mist, then pluck the stars of pointed seeds from the spent blossoms of the cosmos. Like life-forms from some distant planet, each has a surprising shape and exotic beauty, yet all will metamorphose into familiar garden friends. Spread on paper towels, they dry in the warmth of the potting shed for a week or more before we pack them in envelopes, store them in an airtight jar, and pop them into the freezer or refrigerator. Our garden's genes are safe for another season.

While we work, the view through the potting shed windows smolders, then ignites in a blaze of vermilion and gold. Drawn by the drama of color and form, we wander the garden's fringes, gathering branches of maple that drip with winged seed pods, and viburnum clustered with berries as shiny as salmon eggs. We clip leaves from the grapevines, stained like a church window, and cut branches of beauty-berry and sprays of rose hips. Inside the potting shed, we mingle them in baskets with summer's brittle bounty: dried yarrow, fragrant lavender, huge heads of hydrangeas.

drator, or simply stored in a cool dry spot, they will feed and cheer us through the winter.

Meanwhile, we prepare to preserve the fruits of a smaller but equally vital harvest. Working on the potting bench, we scoop seeds

*W*here bottles of milk once chilled, bulbs undergo an artificial winter before being potted up for forcing. In summer months, excess fruits and vegetables find temporary lodgings here.

When the arrangements suit our fancy, we carry them into the house, then turn our attention from last year's flowers to the next. Bulbs have been arriving from our favorite mail-order sources, each one a humble brown-wrapped parcel that holds the soul of spring. They've temporarily been shelved in the potting shed or locked in the arctic confines of the refrigerator, according to our climate. Now we rush to get them into the ground so they can send forth roots before the first hard freeze, or hurry to plant so the daffodils—yellow as marshmallow Easter chicks—will hatch in the brightening days of March. Armed with dibber, trowel, and bulb planter, we struggle to lay oh-so-many bulbs in their soil-lined nests. The air is as crisp as a line-dried sheet; it rejuvenates us as we work.

With back muscles aching, we return to the potting bench to pack tender bulbs of paperwhite narcissus into shallow dishes and pebble-filled saucers. We set weighty amaryllis bulbs in heavy pots, then lower prechilled hyacinth bulbs, like rare gems, into

City gardeners, confined to rooftop, balcony, terrace, and stoop, must pot where weather and space allow.

Before frost kills annual vines such as hops, pick tendrils and twine them around the arc-shaped handles of open baskets. When the vines are dry, use the baskets for arrangements of fall foliage and dried flowers.

fragile settings of glass and water. While winter rages, they will fill our rooms with intoxicating scent and color; for now, they hibernate in a cool dark spot, much like their outdoor cousins.

Then one clear quiet night, after a day as fresh as spring, frost leaves its irrevocable signature, sugaring the remaining pumpkins, wilting the squash vines. It is gone, like smoke, with the first of the sun, but delineates the end of the growing season. There is comfort in its firm decree.

Yet our garden tasks continue. We rake, and rake some more. We roll our cart or wheelbarrow out of the shed or spread a tarp in the middle of vegetables beds, then strip the garden to its winter bones. We pluck the dangling green tomatoes, uproot the rustling foliage, and clean the wire cages. We ferret out the hiding spots of a few dried peppers

*G*ardeners ensure a wintertime display of intoxicating blooms by forcing paperwhite narcissus bulbs, which need no prechilling, late in the fall.

and cut back the withered fronds of the day-lilies. We reap the grayed skeletons of rud-beckia and unearth the corms of tender glad-iolas. The refuse will feed the compost heap until spring; the corms will dry on screens in the potting shed, then rest in a cool dark corner through the winter. Only the kale and Brussels sprouts remain, green outposts in the barren clearing.

"Some garden produce was stored in the shed also—strings of onions, winter squashes, and pumpkins. I recall a large watermelon being kept there one year until it was eaten in November.

—ERNEST A. GOTTS

Finally, on a somber day late in the fall, with the air icy and the ground like iron underfoot, we swaddle the perennials, roses, and other plants with a thick blanket of mulch—protection from winter's indecisive moments—then bring our rakes and forks and wheelbarrows back into the potting shed.

Like the garden, we are ready to rest.

BRINGING IN THE SEEDS

Seed-saving has a wealth of satisfactions, not the least of which is watching plants achieve their only goal in life. Going to seed is not such a bad thing.

Start with easy-to-gather seeds from annuals that don't readily cross with other plants, such as baby's breath, bachelor buttons, calendulas, cosmos, four-o'clocks, foxgloves, hollyhocks, larkspur, morning glories, nasturtiums, nicotiana, and poppies; or from peppers, peas, tomatoes, and beans. Let the plants mature, study them to determine how and when the seeds set and ripen, then harvest.

Clean the seeds of pulp or debris, and dry on paper towels or fine screens for a week or more, even if they appear dry to start with. Package the seeds in small envelopes, label, and store in airtight containers in the refrigerator or freezer until you're ready to begin the seed-to-seed cycle again next spring.

Note: Seeds from hybrids generally will not produce plants with the same characteristics the second time around, and may not sprout at all. It's best to save seeds from plants whose parents were pollinated without man's help (look for seed catalogs that sell "open-pollinated" varieties). Most heirloom and old-fashioned plant varieties are in this category.

WINTER'S HOPE AND GLORY

The first flakes drift like eiderdown from the pewter sky, and we awake to a garden dusted in white. Snow highlights the clipped tops of the boxwoods and shades the underboughs of the smoky spruce. It outlines the branches of the apple, still bearing withered fruit, and silhouettes the towering maple.

Yesterday the garden lay in waste, with all its flaws exposed. Now, like a veiled bride, it stands in chaste perfection. We note its clean geometry: the brick-edged quadrants of the herb garden, the spheres of fragile allium, the upright cones of holly and larch. Its purity both soothes and beckons.

For a week or two, just to look on it is enough. But one gray morning, the starkness fails to satisfy. We pine for the heat of the garden in August, seductive and ripe. The potting shed calls.

We fire up the wood stove or turn the heater to high, and soon our mittens lie next to our garden gloves. Out come sketches of the garden past and present, and with a stool pulled up to the potting bench and a pencil in hand, the frozen garden springs to life.

On paper, we happily discover, summer constraints of time and energy do not apply. There is no weeding, no watering, no troublesome black spot pestering the roses. We move the garden's plants with ease, like flowers in a favorite vase, seeking the perfect marriage of color, texture, and form. We block out space for a bed of bearded iris in watercolor hues, mark a sun-touched spot for a pink-tinged clematis, and draw in a bank of 'Peach Blossom' astilbe. We note new homes for the sea holly, the dou-

ble pink peony, and the campanula. With pencil and eraser we rotate the heavy feeders in the vegetable beds, then shift the lavender and divide the daylilies.

Works of our favorite garden authors, pulled from a nearby shelf, are continually consulted for inspiration and advice. What might thrive in the gap between the hostas and the bleeding heart? Gertrude Jekyll has an idea. What graceful ground cover could replace the carpet of Irish moss that is so difficult to weed? Penelope Hobhouse may have a solution.

With such sages at our sides, our doubts melt away and our inhibitions thaw; no garden plan seems out of reach. An arbor over the front gate, smothered in morning glories. A lathhouse to shelter our transplants of foxglove and columbine. A stone retaining wall, trailing specimens of rock rose and thyme. Never mind the backbreaking weeks it will take us to move the dirt and heft the rocks, which currently form a snow-covered monument to our scavenging skills just behind the shed. Our mental picture of the garden with the wall in place is so vivid

A season's gleaning of seeds, filed briefly in assorted envelopes, will sleep safely in jars until spring arrives.

SEDUCED BY SEEDS

Seed orders are like zucchini; they quickly grow beyond the bounds of reason. To maintain the upper hand, keep these thoughts in mind:

❦ Each year, note what was ordered and what was used. If you ran out of viola seeds or were inundated by peppers last season, adjust your order.

❦ Germination rates for newly purchased seeds generally are high. Unless you plan to sow seed in succession for continuous crops, or naturalize seed over a large area, a single packet of seed usually is ample. Check the catalog for the number of seeds in the packet; some hold only five or ten (plenty if you only need one or two plants), others as many as seven hundred.

❦ Gardeners hate to waste a seed's potential, but it's better to buy too many seeds than too few. If you do have leftovers, store them in an airtight container in the freezer or refrigerator. Check your supply before reordering; plan for a moderate decrease in germination rates the second year.

"*Labels made of lead, and having the number or name stamped in, are very durable, provided they be securely fixed. . . .*"

—ROBERT THOMPSON
THE GARDENER'S ASSISTANT

GARDEN GENEALOGY

We imbibe our garden Latin the way a plant drinks water, with little thought to the process. But without labels and markers, we would soon lose track of the lineage of our plants.

Plant labels have changed little since the early nineteenth century, when estate-garden laborers spent the worst days of winter in the potting shed repainting weather-worn plant names on wooden stakes or cast-iron markers. Such ground-level "name sticks" were in common use, as were wired-on tags of wood, metal, earthenware, bone, or ivory. A more arcane system for noting plant names involved the "tally," a wooden stake notched and scored with a system of marks that corresponded to a number on a printed plant list.

Later in the century, some estate gardeners deployed recyclable metal labels akin to the plastic strips embossed by today's label guns. In his book *The English Flower Garden,* first published in 1883, William Robinson noted that at Kew (the Royal Botanic Gardens) "they now use a lead label of their own stamping." Should the labels "get out of use," he wrote, "it is easy to melt them down and use the metal again."

it seems a fact: work already accomplished.

But we do more in winter than build castles in Spain: figments that won't materialize for months or years to come. On days when the sky is blue and the air is as clear and sharp as glass, we venture forth to shake the snow from the boughs of the evergreens. We prune their fragrant branches, then haul the clippings into the shed and twine them into festive wreaths and garlands. We mingle summer's rosebuds with orris root and essential oils in aromatic potpourri, and make gift tags from the pansies that slumber in the flower press. We shell our beans, content to bide our time until the garden thaws.

On other days the gray returns, somber as a shroud. Warm and safe in the potting shed, but with faltering faith in the surety of the advancing seasons, we dutifully prepare our tools for the pending labors of spring. We sharpen hoes and shovels and massage their tired handles. We scrub empty terra-cotta pots and plastic flats, and wash and dry our cloches. We oil our wheel hoe and push mower, and inscribe the Latin names of plants on sturdy zinc markers and copper tags. Soon, we pray, they will replace the faded nursery labels that lie locked in the frozen earth.

Like a hall closet, the potting shed tends to accumulate odd leftovers from life; here, stamped metal plant labels rest alongside old hardware in the soft light from the shed window.

Garden record-keeping, neglected during active summer months, resumes in fall and winter, particularly as gardeners renew their seed supplies and plan for the coming of spring.

"My mother ran a tight ship. Her potting shed was the nexus of her garden and her gardening. Mine is chaos, though I learned from her. I pot and make a mess in mine and try to garden. I also sit and dream. . . ."

—DAVID M. DAVIS

Then, just when the green of spring seems forever beyond reach, the seed catalogs arrive. They come to the mailbox like life buoys thrown on an icy sea, and we grab them and hold tight. Here is the promise of sun and warmth, the scent of stock, the tang of tomato. Here are old friends and enticing strangers: the life of the garden to come.

Sequestered in the potting shed, with dog-eared catalogs fanned around us and a cup of steaming coffee or cider in hand, we review our plans, closing our eyes to picture the garden at its peak. If we plant ten varieties of heirloom tomatoes, will we really be able to eat them all? Certainly, our taste buds tell us in January. Can we keep up with the zucchini, along with the fiorentino and the patty pan squashes? Of course, we say, conveniently forgetting last year's overwhelming surplus. Five kinds of basil, six types of chili peppers, endless packets of flowering annuals and perennials, four new fruit trees: somehow we envision a place for them all.

We fill out the order forms and send them forth from the potting shed like love letters. Our hopes and dreams for the future are written between the lines.

PAPER GARDENS

Seed catalogs have brightened life for winter-weary gardeners since the early 1800s, when seed sellers and nurserymen first began to grasp the potential of the U.S. Postal Service. But it wasn't until the late 1800s that such pamphlets blossomed into the colorful wish-books we know today. Brightened by vibrant stone lithographs and packed with new "improved" flower and vegetable varieties, agricultural seeds, garden gadgetry, and a wealth of cultural information, some turn-of-the-century seed catalogs boasted as many as two hundred pages. No matter how far from civilization a gardener or farmer lived, if he had a catalog from W. Atlee Burpee, D. Landreth, or D. M. Ferry—and a few cents for postage— 'New White Egg' turnips, 'Joseph's Coat' amaranthus, or 'Extra Early' peas were within reach.

IN THE END, the potting shed is simply a building, nothing more than wood and brick and stone. But in it, our hearts, the pleasures of home, and the glories of the garden merge.

Its practical character eases our garden labors; every tool and potion we need to coax the garden into bloom is close at hand.

Its romantic nature enriches our lives in a more expansive sphere. Here is peace, and beauty, and a sense of purpose. Here is discovery, and increasing knowledge. Here is life, from beginning to end and back to beginning.

Like the garden, the potting shed is fertile ground.

We harvest its bounty for a lifetime.

ACKNOWLEDGMENTS

Like a garden, a book flourishes when it is lovingly fed, weeded, and watered. To each and every person who helped me in those tasks, I offer up my heartfelt thanks.

First, my great appreciation for their research expertise and encouragement to Pamela Jungerberg and Polly Archer (Pacific Grove Library), Rosie Brewer (MOBAC), Sherry Vance (Bailey Hortorium, Cornell University), Marca Woodhams (Smithsonian Horticultural Services Division), and Barbara Pitschel (Strybing Arboretum); as well as to Anne Richards (The Garden History Society), Susan Campbell, and Dr. Christopher Thacker, all of whom generously shared their knowledge of English garden history.

Thanks too, for their rich reminiscences, to Pete Marrow, Ernest A. Gotts, and David M. Davis; to Thomas C. Cooper for his musings in *Odd Lots: Seasonal Notes from a City Gardener* (Henry Holt, 1995); for their knowledge of mystery novels and their on-line aid, to Carol Fleming, Yvonne Lam, I. Pour-El, Valerie Szondy, Shauna Scott, and Dorothy J. Heydt;

for giving me free rein, to Doug Jimerson and Ann Omvig Maine; for their suggestions and enthusiasm, to Ann C. Smith and Marianne Brogan; for her supplemental research and for coming to my rescue, to Mary K. Smith; for his patience, good humor, and unflagging confidence, to Mike Bailey, with whom I plan to garden.

Thanks especially to the generous gardeners who have shared their passions with me throughout the years; to Smith & Hawken, and Kathy Tierney in particular; to Peter Workman and the entire wonderful, welcoming team at Workman Publishing (especially art director Paul Hanson and designer Lauren Graessle, as well as Mary Wilkinson, Lynn Strong, Janice McDonnell and Carbery O'Brien); and most of all to Bonnie Dahan and Sally Kovalchick, without whose vision, inspiration, and careful attentions this book never would have blossomed.

Finally, special thanks to Bill and Joan Smith. You cultivated my love of gardening, history, and books, and for that I am most grateful.

LJS

Heartfelt thanks to all those who kindly opened up their potting sheds on both sides of the Atlantic (especially to those trusting enough to heed our pleas not to have a good tidy-up before we arrived): Debby Albin, Rebecca Coles (Potted Gardens, NYC), Richard Greyser, Lithgow Garden, Nancy McCabe Garden Design, Mark Novak, Helie Robertson, San Domenico School, Christian Shabazian, Susan Sheerer, and Cornelia Sherman. Also to Bonnie Dahan and Anthony Albertus, who made working on the West Coast such a dream.

HP